Original title:
Love Your Work

Copyright © 2024 Creative Arts Management OÜ
All rights reserved.

Author: Tim Wood
ISBN HARDBACK: 978-9916-88-042-5
ISBN PAPERBACK: 978-9916-88-043-2

Passion Ignites the Hours

In the depth of night, I find my fire,
Each flicker burns with fierce desire.
Moments clasped in fervent hold,
Time dissolves, the stories unfold.

Every heartbeat is music, profound,
Echoing softly, a love unbound.
With each step taken, spirits align,
Passion ignites, a force divine.

Crafting Dreams with Every Stroke

Canvas stretched, the colors sing,
Whispers of hope, the brush takes wing.
Each stroke a journey, wild and free,
Crafting the visions that live in me.

The palette dances, shades collide,
Imaginary worlds, where dreams reside.
With patience unfolding, the magic grows,
Artistry blossoms, every heart knows.

Embracing the Daily Grind

Morning light spills, a brand new day,
Chasing the rhythm, come what may.
Each task a step, a mountain to climb,
Embracing the grind, one moment in time.

Fingers dance on the keys of fate,
Building tomorrow, it's never too late.
Strength in persistence, dreams lace the air,
In the daily grind, we find our flair.

Whispers of Dedication

A quiet vow beneath the stars,
In every challenge, every scar.
Whispers of dedication blend with night,
Fueling the spirit, igniting the light.

Through trials faced, resilience grows,
Each stumble a lesson, a seed that sows.
With hearts aligned, our voices soar,
In whispers of dedication, we crave more.

Committed to the Craft

In shadows cast by the fading light,
Hands toil on through the day and night.
With every stroke, and every thread,
Passion whispers where dreams are bred.

Chisels dance on the weary stone,
Each mark speaks of a heart well-known.
Through struggle and patience, skills refine,
In the forge of time, their spirits shine.

A Journey of Service

Under the banner of selflessness bright,
Stepping forth into the night.
With every hand reached, and every care,
The fabric of hope is woven there.

In fields of people, love must grow,
Giving strength where the rivers flow.
Each smile shared, a spark of grace,
Together we light this sacred space.

The Pulse of Purpose

In the heartbeat of dreams that dare,
Echoes rattle the stagnant air.
With every step, intentions unfold,
Stories of courage, softly told.

A compass guides through paths unknown,
Mapping journeys that lead us home.
In the rhythm of loss and gain,
Purpose flows like the gentle rain.

Heartfelt Pursuits

In the quiet hum of early dawn,
The soul awakens to journey on.
With whispers of wishes, stars ignite,
Chasing the shadows of fleeting light.

Every laugh shared, a precious gem,
A tapestry rich, we weave again.
Through trials faced and fears set free,
Heartfelt pursuits make us truly see.

The Gift of Grit

In shadows deep, we find our flame,
A spark ignites, no fear, no shame.
Through trials faced, we rise anew,
With strength found in the fires we strew.

The path is rough, the hill is steep,
But promise blooms where hearts don't weep.
We gather stones, a sturdy wall,
With grit, we learn to stand and crawl.

Painting Life's Canvas

With every brush, a story told,
Colors dance, both bright and bold.
From muted tones to vibrant sights,
We craft our dreams, we chase the lights.

Each stroke's a choice, a path to claim,
We weave our joys, we shade our pain.
In every hue, reflections lie,
Our canvas breathes, it learns to fly.

Embracing Every Task

With open hands, we greet the day,
Each task a chance, a role to play.
From small to grand, we dive right in,
With purpose found, the journey begins.

In toil we learn, in grit we grow,
The seeds we plant, with care, we sow.
With every challenge, we rise and stand,
Embracing life, hand in hand.

The Alchemy of Purpose

In silence deep, the heart will yearn,
For meaning found, for truth to learn.
We gather dreams and hopes like gold,
Through trials faced, our stories unfold.

From leaden days, we shape the fire,
Transmute our doubts, and dare aspire.
With purpose bright, we light our way,
In alchemy, our souls betray.

Embracing Challenges

In shadows deep, we find our light,
Through trials faced, we learn to fight.
Each setback bends but does not break,
With every step, new ground we make.

With hearts ablaze, we take the road,
Unbowed we stand, our spirits strode.
For in each struggle, wisdom grows,
And in our journey, courage flows.

The Spirit of Creation

Awake within, the muse does call,
With every spark, we rise and fall.
Colors dance upon the page,
Each stroke a whisper, breaking cage.

In silence deep, ideas bloom,
A symphony within the room.
With hands that shape, and hearts that dream,
We weave our truths into the seam.

Transforming Work into Art

In the mundane, beauty hides,
Each task we take, our passion rides.
With careful hands, we mold and craft,
Turning the dull into a draft.

As deadlines loom, we find our fire,
In every challenge, we aspire.
From labor's grind, we rise anew,
Finding purpose in what we do.

The Warmth of Dedication

Through endless nights and tireless days,
In quiet strength, our spirit stays.
For love of craft, we give our all,
In every rise, we answer the call.

With every breath, commitment grows,
In heart and hand, the passion flows.
In unity, we choose to stand,
For in dedication, we find our land.

Heartbeats in the Office

In the glow of screens, we meet,
Fingers dance on keyboards fleet.
A coffee break, a sigh, a laugh,
Moments shared, our daily path.

Whispers linger in each space,
The hustle quickens, we embrace.
Dreams and deadlines intertwine,
In the heart of work, we shine.

The Symphony of Labor

In cadence, tasks flow like song,
Together, we all belong.
Voices rise and fall, a blend,
Each note brings us closer, friend.

Pages turn and pens do glide,
In harmony, we decide.
Every challenge faced with grace,
Creating a timeless place.

Finding Joy in the Mundane

A daily grind, yet laughter's found,
In the hum of life, we're bound.
Moments small, yet bright and clear,
Finding joy, we persevere.

Clocks may tick, but hearts ignite,
In tasks routine, our spirits light.
With every chore, a smile's reign,
Transforming work from dull to gain.

Building Bridges with Each Task

With every project, we connect,
A bridge we build, we intersect.
Collaboration shapes our day,
In unity, we find our way.

Tools in hand, we craft and mold,
Stories shared, ambitions bold.
Together stronger, side by side,
In every effort, hearts abide.

A Canvas of Commitment

With each stroke of steadfast brush,
We paint our dreams with vibrant hues.
A canvas stretched, our hearts we flush,
In every drop, our love renews.

Through trials faced, we find our way,
Each color tells a story bold.
In shadows cast, there shines the day,
A masterpiece of truth unfolds.

When Ambition Meets Affection

In the dance of dreams, we twirl,
Ambition's fire lighting the night.
With gentle hands, love's flags unfurl,
Together, we reach for our flight.

With passion's push, we take the leap,
And in that jump, our hearts entwine.
In every promise, faith runs deep,
For in this journey, love will shine.

The Art of Meaningful Endeavors

Each step we take, a brush in hand,
We sculpt our paths, both bold and bright.
With purpose clear, like grains of sand,
We mold our lives, ignite the light.

In depth of heart, intentions rush,
Through hurdles faced, we shape our fate.
With every stroke, we build and brush,
In labor's love, we celebrate.

Cherishing Every Challenge

Each challenge faced is but a gift,
A chance to grow, to learn, to rise.
With every struggle, spirits shift,
In trials tough, we seek the prize.

Through storms we walk, hand in hand,
With laughter, tears, a woven thread.
In every setback, we will stand,
For in our hearts, courage is fed.

The Aura of Aspiration

In dreams we find our path anew,
With courage bright, we push on through.
Each step we take, towards the light,
With hearts ablaze, we soar in flight.

Beyond the clouds, our hopes will rise,
We'll paint the world with vibrant skies.
Awake the fire, embrace the call,
For in our spirit, we will not fall.

The Spirit of Service

With open hands and hearts so wide,
We lend a hand, we stand beside.
In every kindness, seeds we sow,
A ripple spreads, our love will grow.

To lift a soul, to share a smile,
We walk this path, though it's not a mile.
In every gesture, grace we find,
Together strong, in heart and mind.

Crafting Joy

In laughter shared, our spirits dance,
We weave together every chance.
With simple joys, we build a way,
To light the world, to bright each day.

In fleeting moments, joy we frame,
With colors bright, we fan the flame.
Through trials faced, we find our cheer,
In every heartbeat, love draws near.

The Essence of Engagement

In every voice, a story told,
With open hearts, we break the mold.
We listen close, we seek to learn,
In shared connections, passion burns.

Through dialogues, we bridge the gap,
In every smile, a shared map.
Together we rise, together we stand,
In unity's grasp, we take a hand.

Harmony of Hands

Hands entwined, a gentle touch,
Whispers of dreams, meaning so much.
Silent language, woven so tight,
In the embrace, everything feels right.

Crafting moments, both soft and grand,
Together we rise, together we stand.
In the rhythm of life, we find our way,
Harmony building, day after day.

Every gesture speaks from the heart,
Creating a bond that will never part.
In the dance of existence, we sway,
Two souls united, come what may.

Soulful Endeavors

Chasing the light, beyond the dawn,
Where dreams awaken, and fears are gone.
Every step taken, pure and true,
In soulful endeavors, just me and you.

Through the valleys, over the hills,
Our spirits twine in joyous thrills.
With open hearts, we seek and find,
Life's sweetest treasures, intertwined.

A journey crafted with every breath,
In the embrace of life, there's no death.
For in our passions, we come alive,
In soulful pursuits, together we thrive.

The Beauty of Commitment

Bound by promises, hearts in sync,
In every moment, a shared link.
Through joy and sorrow, we will stay,
The beauty of commitment lights the way.

With each sunrise, a vow renewed,
In quiet strength, our love is stewed.
Hand in hand, we forge our fate,
In unity, we celebrate.

Through storms we weather, through trials we pass,
With every glance, our reflections amassed.
A tapestry woven, threads of gold,
The beauty of commitment, a story told.

In Pursuit of Joy

In a world of dreams, we chase the light,
With open hearts, we take our flight.
Every laughter shared, every tear,
In pursuit of joy, we draw you near.

Through fields of wonder and skies so blue,
We find our bliss, me and you.
In the little moments, pure delight,
In pursuit of joy, the world feels right.

With every heartbeat, a dance unfolds,
Life's sweetest tales in whispers told.
In the journey, together we play,
In pursuit of joy, come what may.

A Symphony of Skills

In the workshop, hands will meet,
Crafting dreams where visions greet.
Each tool sings a different tune,
Harmony beneath the moon.

Minds at work, ideas flow,
Bringing life to what we know.
Colors burst and shapes collide,
Joy and passion intertwined.

Create to build, to mend, to grow,
Every effort, every show.
A dance of craft, a song of art,
A symphony that won't depart.

Sowing Passion

In the garden, seeds are sown,
Tender hands in soil are grown.
Water whispers, sun's embrace,
Life unfurls with gentle grace.

Dreams take root, and love will bloom,
Nurtured hearts dispel the gloom.
Fruits of labor, sweet reward,
Harvest whispers of accord.

Nature's rhythm, pulse of time,
Growing stronger, love will climb.
Sowing passion, letting go,
Life's rich tapestry will glow.

The Light in Labor

With every dawn, the world awakes,
Hands that toil, the fire makes.
Chasing shadows, bright and bold,
The light in labor turns to gold.

Struggles faced, lessons learned,
Through the storms, our spirits burned.
Resilience shines in darkest night,
Illuminating paths of light.

Every heartbeat, every sigh,
Etched in time as dreams comply.
We labor on, with hope so bright,
Finding strength in shared delight.

Embracing the Rhythm

In the heart of the night, we sway,
With every beat, we find our way.
Whispers of joy in every breath,
Together we dance, forgetting death.

Step by step, we lose the fear,
In the rhythm, our souls are clear.
Every turn, a chance to grow,
Embracing the rhythm, letting go.

Beneath the stars, our spirits fly,
In this moment, we touch the sky.
The world fades, just you and me,
In the song of life, we are free.

With every movement, passion ignites,
Our dreams entwined, like day and nights.
In the embrace of the music's sound,
Forever together, our hearts are bound.

In the Flow of Passion

In the morning light, we rise anew,
Chasing dreams, both bold and true.
With every heartbeat, flames burn bright,
In the flow of passion, we ignite.

Brush strokes blend on canvas wide,
A dance of colors, side by side.
Each moment whispers, love's sweet grace,
In this flow, we find our place.

With fervor strong, we break the mold,
Stories of life, together told.
In every challenge, we will strive,
With passion's fire, we come alive.

Through storms and winds, we boldly sail,
The compass points, our love won't fail.
In the flow of passion, time stands still,
With every heartbeat, a shared will.

Crafting Dreams

In quiet corners, visions form,
With gentle hands, we break the norm.
Molding hope from clay of night,
Crafting dreams, we chase the light.

Every thought a brush in hand,
Painting futures, a life so grand.
With every stroke, our spirits soar,
Crafting dreams, forevermore.

In whispered secrets, plans unfold,
Together daring, brave and bold.
Through shadows deep, we find our way,
Crafting dreams, come what may.

With open hearts, we share our truths,
The laughter echoes, fires of youth.
In unity, our spirits beam,
Together always, we craft our dream.

A Dance with Dedication

With every step, a promise made,
In the spotlight, fears do fade.
All it takes is a single chance,
In this life, we learn to dance.

Through the trials, we push on through,
Each new beat brings something new.
With grace and strength, we find our stance,
In dedication, we advance.

In the mirror, our spirits glow,
Reflection of love, a steady flow.
With every fall, we rise again,
A dance with dedication, free from pain.

Through open hearts, we share the fire,
With every move, we climb higher.
In this dance, we find our fate,
With dedication, we celebrate.

Fired by Inspiration

A spark ignites within my heart,
Ideas dance, refusing to part.
Dreams awaken, colors bloom,
In this chaos, visions loom.

With every thought, new worlds I trace,
Creativity finds its space.
Whispers of passion, bold and bright,
Guide my hand through the night.

In silence, echoes start to rise,
Thoughts like stars fill endless skies.
On wings of hope, my spirit flies,
Fired by inspiration, it never dies.

Heartstrings of Labor

Hands that toil beneath the sun,
Each drop of sweat, a battle won.
Crafting dreams with every stroke,
In every test, new strengths evoke.

Patience weaves a gentle thread,
Through trials faced and words unsaid.
In labor's dance, stories unfold,
Heartstrings bound in threads of gold.

For every burden, a lesson learned,
Every challenge, passion burned.
With steadfast hearts, we rise again,
In unity, our spirits mend.

The Art of Giving

A simple act, a tender touch,
In giving, we receive so much.
Kindness blooms from open hands,
In every heart, true love expands.

Gifts not wrapped, but meant to share,
In moments spent, in earnest care.
Each smile exchanged, a spark of light,
In the shadows, we shine bright.

The art of giving knows no bounds,
In laughter found, in joyous sounds.
In every heartbeat, love we send,
Creating bonds that never end.

Radiance in Routine

In the rhythm of each day,
Familiar steps, a gentle sway.
Morning light, a soft embrace,
In routines, we find our place.

With every task, a chance to gleam,
In the mundane, we can dream.
As seconds pass, we find our song,
In little things, we all belong.

Through cycles spun in endless ways,
We discover joy in simple days.
Radiance lies in what we do,
In routine's warmth, our hearts break through.

Flourishing in Focus

In the garden where dreams grow bright,
Seeds of purpose take their flight.
Nurtured by the sun's warm grace,
Blooms of passion find their place.

With every raindrop, hope ignites,
Chasing shadows of restless nights.
Each petal whispers, soft and clear,
The beauty of a vision near.

Roots entwined in fertile ground,
Strength in silence all around.
A tranquil mind, a heart at ease,
Guides the spirit like the breeze.

In this haven, life unfolds,
Stories waiting to be told.
Flourishing in focus, we stride,
With courage blooming deep inside.

The Melody of Ambition

Notes of dreams, they softly play,
Harmonies guide us on our way.
With every step, the rhythm grows,
A pulse of strength that flows and flows.

Chasing visions, bright and bold,
In pursuit of moments yet untold.
Melodies of hope intertwine,
Daring us to cross the line.

In the echo of desire's song,
We find the courage to belong.
Strides may falter, yet we rise,
With passion lighting up the skies.

The melody of ambition calls,
Through quiet nights and crowded halls.
With hearts united in the dance,
We seize the day, we take the chance.

Heartfelt Endeavors

In the quiet, we plant our seeds,
Tending to the heart's deep needs.
With gentle hands and open minds,
We sow the love that nature finds.

Through trials faced and lessons learned,
A tapestry of courage turned.
With every stitch, we weave our fate,
In heartfelt endeavors, we create.

For in the struggle, growth does bloom,
From shadows deep, dispels the gloom.
A dance of dreams, both near and far,
Guides our path like a shining star.

With open arms, we greet the day,
Embracing life in every way.
Heartfelt endeavors, strong and true,
Are moments that lead us to renew.

Echoes of Enthusiasm

Voices rise with fervent cheer,
Echoes of enthusiasm near.
In every laughter, joy unfolds,
A tapestry of life retold.

With every challenge, spirits soar,
Pushing boundaries, seeking more.
The spark ignites as dreams align,
Filling hearts with hope divine.

In the dance of life's embrace,
We find our rhythm, find our place.
Together strong, we chase the light,
In echoes of enthusiasm bright.

Every heartbeat tells the tale,
Of journeys taken, of wind and sail.
Hand in hand, we greet the dawn,
And celebrate the dreams reborn.

Each Step a New Possibility

With every step, the path unfolds,
New doors await, with stories untold.
Fear not the fall, nor shadows cast,
For in each stumble, we find the vast.

Hope blooms bright in the unknown,
Each choice we make, a seed is sown.
The journey calls, so take the chance,
Dance through the doubt, embrace the dance.

With open hearts, we chase the sun,
A world of wonders has just begun.
In every heartbeat, a whisper grows,
Each step a chance, as courage shows.

So step by step, let dreams ignite,
In every moment, find the light.
Embrace the journey, let it be,
Each step a new possibility.

Crafting the Life We Envision

With brush in hand, we craft our art,
Each stroke reflects our beating heart.
Dreams take shape on this canvas wide,
In colors bold, we choose our stride.

The blueprint holds our secret plans,
A vision grows beyond mere sands.
Through trials faced and laughter shared,
A tapestry of life is dared.

Brick by brick, we shape the ground,
In every challenge, wisdom found.
The life we envision is within reach,
With every lesson, life will teach.

So let us weave a tale of hope,
With threads of courage, we will cope.
Embracing change, we now begin,
Crafting our lives, let dreams spin.

Radiance in Routine

In morning light, routine awakes,
With coffee brewed and simple cakes.
The sun spills gold on every task,
In mundane moments, joy we'll unmask.

With breath so deep, we anchor here,
In every action, love draws near.
Through rhythmic days, our spirits soar,
Finding beauty in the mundane's core.

As hours pass, we find our flow,
In gentle waves, the heart will know.
Each task we do, a spark ignites,
Radiance glows through simple sights.

So cherish routine, a comforting friend,
Within its grasp, our souls extend.
In every repetition, life's embrace,
Radiance blooms in every space.

The Melodies of Meaningful Labor

With hands that toil and hearts that sing,
We find our joy in every spring.
In building dreams, we find our pace,
The melodies in work we grace.

Each task we take, a note is played,
A symphony that won't soon fade.
Through sweat and smile, purpose grows,
In meaningful labor, our passion flows.

As challenges rise, our voices blend,
In harmony, we'll find the end.
Each laborer's song, together we chant,
In every struggle, a resounding grant.

So dance through work, embrace the strain,
For in this labor, joy will reign.
With every melody, our lives align,
The melodies of meaningful labor, divine.

Threads of Passion Weaved Together

In the tapestry of dreams, we thread,
Colors vibrant, stories unsaid.
With each stitch, our hearts align,
Crafting moments, pure and divine.

Embers flicker, the fire's glow,
United paths where love can flow.
Through laughter, tears, we intertwine,
Creating a bond that's truly divine.

The fabric of life, in every hue,
Woven with hopes, forever true.
In the loom of time, we find our way,
Together we shine, come what may.

In the patterns of joy, we discover,
Threads of passion that softly cover.
With every heartbeat, we grow strong,
In the symphony of love, we belong.

The Luminescence of Purposeful Days

Morning breaks with golden beams,
Awakening hearts, igniting dreams.
Each hour unfolds with grace divine,
Guiding our steps, a grand design.

In the pursuit of a radiant goal,
Purpose ignites the yearning soul.
With every task, we leave our mark,
Lighting paths, igniting the spark.

Wonders bloom in the in-between,
Finding magic in moments unseen.
With passion driving our every way,
We embrace the light of purposeful days.

As dusk settles and stars align,
We cherish the hours that intertwine.
In the fabric of time, we find our place,
In the luminescence, we embrace.

Portraits of Perseverance

In the canvas of life, every hue,
Faces reflect the journeys we pursue.
Strength in struggle, beauty in pain,
Every stroke tells of loss and gain.

Through storms that test our very soul,
Emerging giants, once feeling small.
Resilient hearts, with stories to share,
In portraits of hope, we lay us bare.

Moments of doubt, the shadows cast,
Yet we rise up, break free from the past.
With every challenge, we grow anew,
Painting dreams with a vibrant view.

We carry the weight of our deep scars,
But they shine bright, like guiding stars.
In every portrait, courage displayed,
In perseverance, our fears allayed.

Finding Light in the Work

In the grind of daily tasks, we strive,
Seeking purpose that keeps us alive.
Through sweat and toil, dreams ignite,
Finding meaning in the day and night.

Every challenge, a step toward grace,
In the rhythm of work, we find our place.
With passion's fire lighting the way,
We embrace the dawn of each new day.

In the labor of love, hearts align,
Creating wonders, divine design.
With hands that build and minds that dream,
We find the light in every beam.

In the journey's heart, we gain our worth,
Celebrating the beauty of our earth.
With every moment, we strive to see,
Finding light in the work we seek to be.

Joy in the Journey

Step by step, we wander wide,
With every turn, new dreams reside.
Laughter echoes, hearts align,
In every moment, joy we find.

Through winding roads, the sun will shine,
In shadows deep, the stars still twine.
Each twist and curve, a tale unfolds,
In every journey, life retold.

Embrace the path, both fierce and mild,
In every heartbeat, joy is wild.
Adventure calls, we must abide,
With open hearts, we take the ride.

A tapestry of sights and sounds,
In every step, true magic grounds.
Together we explore the views,
In joy we find our vibrant hues.

Threads of Inspiration

In whispers soft, ideas bloom,
Like morning light dispelling gloom.
A spark ignites, a thought takes flight,
In threads of hope, we weave our sight.

From nature's breath, to worlds unseen,
In every corner, beauty gleaned.
Connections spark, and hearts embrace,
In fleeting moments, we find grace.

Inspire the soul with whispered dreams,
Through laughter shared and silver beams.
Each story told, a thread so fine,
We stitch our lives, with joy entwined.

The tapestry of life we weave,
In every heart, we can believe.
Through passion's flame, we light the way,
Threads of inspiration guide our stay.

The Pulse of Progress

With every heartbeat, change begins,
In struggles faced, our strength within.
The road is long, yet we persist,
With hope alive, we can't resist.

Each challenge met with courage bold,
In every trial, new stories told.
Momentum builds, a fervent drive,
In each small act, we come alive.

Steps forward take us to new heights,
Innovate, create, ignite the nights.
With vision clear, we set our sights,
In unison, we change our rights.

Through every pulse, we stand as one,
In progress found, our hearts have spun.
Together we can shape our fate,
With passion strong, we cultivate.

Cultivating Creativity

In gardens rich where ideas grow,
With patience nurtured, seeds we sow.
Through trials faced and joys we share,
Creativity blooms, beyond compare.

With colors bold, we paint the sky,
In every stroke, our spirits fly.
A canvas wide, our dreams take form,
In this wild space, we all transform.

Imagination flows like streams,
In every thought, we chase our dreams.
Building worlds, we find our voice,
In every heartbeat, we rejoice.

With open minds and hearts so free,
We cultivate our legacy.
In every spark, a light we find,
Creativity, our hearts entwined.

Harmony in Hustle

In the noise of city life,
We find moments of peace.
With each step we take,
Our hopes begin to increase.

Amidst the rush and the race,
A melody starts to swell.
The heart learns to keep pace,
In this story we tell.

Like rivers that intertwine,
Our paths align with grace.
Working hard, yet we shine,
Together we find our place.

In every toil and trial,
A harmony can unfold.
With dreams that stretch a mile,
In unity, we are bold.

The Poetry of Progress

Each step forward we take,
Is a verse in our song.
In the quest for what's great,
We find where we belong.

With pages yet unturned,
New stories come to light.
In lessons that we've learned,
We soar to greater height.

Brick by brick, we will build,
A future we hold dear.
With passion, hearts are filled,
Chasing dreams without fear.

Through struggles, we will grow,
In the dance of our time.
With every ebb and flow,
We write our own rhyme.

Driven by Dreams

In the quiet of the night,
Dreams whisper soft and low.
Fueling our inner fight,
They guide us as we go.

The stars above us gleam,
Lighting paths yet unknown.
With courage, we will dream,
And venture out alone.

Every challenge we face,
Brings wisdom and intent.
In the rush of the race,
Our spirit won't relent.

With passion as our guide,
And purpose on the rise,
In our hearts, we confide,
For dreams are endless skies.

Crafting the Future

With hands that mold the clay,
We shape what's yet to be.
In every choice we lay,
Lies the heart of our decree.

The canvas wide and vast,
Awaits our brush of fate.
We paint shadows and cast,
A vision bright and great.

Through trials, we create,
A narrative of change.
In unity, we navigate,
Together, we are brave.

With dreams that intertwine,
And hope that will abide,
In crafting, we define,
The world, where we'll reside.

Devotion in Motion

In the dance of dawn's first light,
Hearts entwined, souls take flight.
Every step, a silent vow,
In devotion's grip, we bow.

With each beat, a rhythm grows,
In the hush, a passion flows.
Hand in hand, we find our way,
Guided by the love we display.

Through the trials, we shall run,
Finding strength in hearts as one.
In this journey, side by side,
With devotion, we abide.

As twilight fades into the night,
Our spirits soar, forever bright.
In motion, we will always stay,
Bound by love, come what may.

Whispers of Fulfillment

In the quiet, dreams arise,
Softly spoken, like the skies.
Every wish, a gentle sigh,
Whispers of the heart nearby.

Through the shadows, hopes will weave,
In the night, we dare believe.
Filling spaces, making whole,
The whispers cradle every soul.

Moments shared, and laughter rings,
In their grace, our spirit sings.
Each encounter, a step ahead,
Guided softly where we tread.

Fulfillment blooms in tender care,
In our truths, we lay it bare.
With every whisper, fears take flight,
Together, we embrace the light.

The Joy of Creation

From a spark, the canvas glows,
In the stillness, passion flows.
Every stroke, a heartbeat true,
Creation sings in all we do.

Colors dance and rhythms rise,
In the moment, freedom lies.
Crafting visions, bold and bright,
Illuminating our own light.

With our hands, we shape the day,
In this beauty, find our way.
Every dream is a work of art,
A reflection of the heart.

In creation, we find our voice,
In every choice, we embrace rejoice.
With each moment, new ideas bloom,
In the joy of life, we consume.

Bound by Purpose

In the stillness, aim is clear,
Every step, we conquer fear.
Bound together, hand in hand,
With a purpose we will stand.

Through the storms, we find our way,
In each challenge, bright we stay.
Driven by the dreams we share,
Bound by purpose, hearts laid bare.

With a vision, we ignite,
In the darkness, we are light.
Nothing can our spirit sever,
In this bond, we are forever.

Through the journey, wide and vast,
In our truth, we'll hold steadfast.
Purpose leads us, ever strong,
Together, we will right the wrong.

Threads of Aspiration

In dreams we weave our hopes so bright,
Each thread a whisper in the night.
With courage strong, we stitch and sew,
Creating paths for hearts to grow.

Through struggles faced, we find our way,
A tapestry of each hard day.
With every knot, a story told,
A future bright, a heart of gold.

As threads entwine, we rise as one,
Beneath the moon, beneath the sun.
The journey's long, the end unclear,
But step by step, we conquer fear.

Together strong, our dreams take flight,
In unity, we shine so bright.
With threads of hope, we craft our fate,
In every heart, a spark innate.

A Tapestry of Meaning

In colors bold, we find our way,
Each moment threads the light of day.
A fabric rich with life's design,
In every stitch, our hearts align.

With every challenge that we face,
We weave new patterns, find our place.
Through laughter shared and sorrows deep,
A tapestry, our dreams to keep.

In quiet corners, stories grow,
Each loop a tale, each flow a glow.
Embracing all that life can bring,
In unity, our voices sing.

Together, we compose this art,
Each single thread a vital part.
In every weave, a bond we find,
A tapestry of heart and mind.

The Dance of Productivity

In morning light, our spirits rise,
With purpose clear and open eyes.
We move with grace, our steps aligned,
A rhythm found in heart and mind.

Through tasks at hand, we find our flow,
With energy that starts to grow.
Collaboration brings us near,
Each voice a note, each thought sincere.

We dance through challenges with glee,
Transforming work to artistry.
In every move, a chance to shine,
With passion strong, our goals define.

As evening falls, our tasks complete,
We celebrate, our joy replete.
In every dance, our dreams pursue,
With one another, we break through.

Rooted in Passion

From deep within, our fires ignite,
With every heartbeat, hopes take flight.
A passion fierce, a guiding star,
Through every shadow, near or far.

In fields of dreams, we plant our seeds,
Nurtured by love, our hearts' deep needs.
With every challenge, we will grow,
In every moment, passion's glow.

With roots so strong, we stand our ground,
In unity, our voices sound.
Through storms that rage and winds that howl,
Our passion's flame, we will avow.

And when the sun begins to set,
We gather dreams, we won't forget.
For rooted deep in love's embrace,
We find our strength, our sacred space.

Chasing the Flame

In the night, a flicker glows,
Dancing shadows, wild and free.
Hearts ignited with longing knows,
The path ahead is meant to be.

Through the darkness, dreams collide,
With whispered hopes that never wane.
Fires of passion as our guide,
We run forth to chase the flame.

With every step, the warmth we seek,
Fueling lives with fervent cheer.
In the journey, we grow less meek,
For the flame burns bright and clear.

Now we stand, together bold,
In unity, we lift our name.
With each story, brightly told,
Forever chasing that same flame.

The Power of Purpose

In shadows deep, a whisper calls,
Guiding hearts through stormy gales.
Purpose strong, it never stalls,
A beacon bright that never pales.

With every rise, we find our way,
Through trials faced and burdens borne.
In every night, there comes a day,
Where dreams awaken, newly born.

Like rivers flow, our spirits soar,
In alignment, we take our stand.
With purpose deep, we strive for more,
Together, we create our land.

In unity, we break the chains,
Harnessing strength from all around.
With purpose clear, we'll face the pains,
And rise again, forever bound.

The Luster of Labor

In calloused hands, the stories lie,
Of sweat and toil, of hopes and dreams.
With every task, we reach the sky,
Crafting futures in golden beams.

The grind may wear, yet spirits lift,
Through dedication, we find our way.
Each effort made, a precious gift,
In labor's light, we find our play.

From dawn to dusk, we cast our fate,
With every heartbeat, challenges sway.
In unity, we celebrate,
The luster of labor in our day.

For sweat brings forth a harvest sweet,
In every trial, we grow strong.
Together, we embrace our feat,
And sing the labor's joyful song.

Inspired Innovation

Bright ideas in minds take flight,
Like sparks igniting in the night.
With dreams unleashed, we chase the new,
Creating wonders, bold and true.

In every corner, visions form,
A surge of change, a blazing storm.
We break the mold and redefine,
The world awakens, so divine.

With hands that shape and hearts aligned,
The pulse of progress is enshrined.
Inspired steps, we march ahead,
With innovation, hope is spread.

Through trials faced, we stand as one,
In unity, our work is spun.
With passion fierce, we'll rise above,
Embracing change, we thrive on love.

Blooming Where You Are Planted

In the soil of your heart, sow the seeds,
Nurture them with love, fulfill their needs.
With every drop of rain, let hope arise,
Watch as your spirit begins to surprise.

Embrace the light, let it shine through,
Even in shadows, find what is true.
Each moment a chance, each breath anew,
Blooming where you are, just as you do.

The roots you establish will guide your way,
In the toughest of storms, they choose to stay.
Lift your head high, let your colors unfold,
In every sunrise, your story is told.

From the cracks in the pavement, flowers grow,
Resilience is beauty, even in woe.
So stand strong and firm, let your essence be,
Blooming where you are, wild and free.

The Dance of Purpose

In the rhythm of life, find your own beat,
Every step you take, with joy you greet.
Let your heart lead, feel the music play,
In this dance of purpose, find your way.

Twirl through the challenges, glide with ease,
Every stumble a lesson, every pause a breeze.
As you move with intention, let passion ignite,
In the dance of purpose, you'll shine bright.

With friends by your side, together you'll sway,
Creating a symphony, come what may.
In every heartbeat, celebrate your aim,
The dance of purpose, never the same.

So take a deep breath, and let go of fear,
In this joyful journey, your path is clear.
Embrace every moment, let your spirit fly,
In the dance of purpose, you'll touch the sky.

Spirit of Creation Unshackled

Unfurl your wings, let the wildness out,
Embrace the chaos, dispel the doubt.
In the realm of creation, set your mind free,
The spirit unshackled is where you'll see.

With each brush stroke, let your soul sing,
A melody of colors, the joy you bring.
Crafting dreams with laughter, bold and bright,
In the spirit of creation, find your light.

Chase the shadows, let your brilliance shine,
In every mistake, there lies a design.
The whispers of genius dance in the air,
Spirit unshackled, breaking through despair.

So sketch your visions, let them flow loud,
Walk your own path, stand tall and proud.
In the tapestry woven, your truth is displayed,
The spirit of creation will never fade.

Harvesting Happiness in Every Effort

Plant the seeds of joy with every deed,
In the garden of life, love is your creed.
Nurture each moment, let kindness grow,
Harvesting happiness, let gratitude flow.

In the sweat of your brow, find sweet reward,
Every challenge faced, a chance to move forward.
Sow the laughter, reap the smiles that appear,
Harvesting happiness, year after year.

With hands wide open, embrace what you find,
In the beauty of giving, hearts intertwined.
As you gather blessings, let worries cease,
Harvesting happiness, your soul's release.

So tend to your garden, each flower a sign,
In the effort of love, let your spirit align.
With every small act, let joy take its place,
Harvesting happiness, a warm embrace.

Composing a Life of Significance

In shadows deep, we weave our way,
With dreams alight, we greet the day.
Each choice a note in time's grand song,
We find our place where we belong.

Through trials hard, and moments sweet,
We carve our path, embrace the beat.
With courage bold, we rise and soar,
Each chapter penned, we need no more.

In love and loss, we shape our tale,
With every breath, we will not fail.
A life of worth, with purpose clear,
In harmony, we draw our peers.

Together bound, our spirits bright,
We compose a life, a wondrous sight.
Each memory a cherished gift,
In significance, our hearts uplift.

Harmony in Hard Work

With calloused hands, we toil each day,
In sweat and grit, we find our way.
The rhythm strong, like nature's tune,
We labor hard, from morn to noon.

Each task a step, each effort small,
We build our dreams, we heed the call.
Through trials faced, each lesson learned,
In harmony, our passions burned.

With focus sharp, we chase the light,
In darkest hours, we find our might.
The fruits of labor, sweet and ripe,
In unity, we form the type.

Together strong, our goals align,
In hard work's grace, our stars will shine.
With every beat, our spirits grow,
In harmony, our hopes will flow.

Passion's Embrace

In every heart, a fire ignites,
With passion's song, our soul delights.
We chase our dreams, with fervor pure,
In loving arms, we find our cure.

Each moment spent, a treasure sought,
In endeavors rich, our battles fought.
Through threads of hope, our spirits weave,
In passion's grasp, we learn to believe.

With visions clear, we rise anew,
In every breath, the joy we pursue.
Creating worlds where dreams take flight,
In passion's embrace, we find our light.

Together we dance, in sweet accord,
With every pulse, our hearts restored.
In vibrant hues, our paths entwined,
In passion's hold, our souls aligned.

The Heart of Craft

In gentle hands, we shape and mold,
With voices soft, our stories told.
Each stroke of skill, a testament,
In artistry, our love is spent.

Through trials faced, and patience learned,\nIn every piece, a passion burned.
Creating wonders, both bold and fine,
In the heart of craft, our spirits shine.

With every weave, and every line,
A bond is forged, a true design.
In craftsmanship, our souls connect,
With timeless grace, we choose to reflect.

Together we stand, united strong,
With every task, we all belong.
In heart's embrace, our dreams are cast,
In the heart of craft, our joys amassed.

Creating with Conviction

With every stroke, a dream unfolds,
A vision bold, in colors told.
Hands that shape with fervent grace,
In this craft, a sacred space.

Ideas spark like stars at night,
Foundations built on pure delight.
Each creation sings a tune,
Echoes of a heart's monsoon.

Through struggles faced and doubts amassed,
The journey forged, we hold steadfast.
For every flaw, a lesson learned,
In passion's fire, our spirits burned.

So create with heart, let courage lead,
In every thought, plant a seed.
With conviction strong, let moments thrive,
In this art, we feel alive.

The Light of Dedication

In quiet hours, dreams take flight,
Fueled by the glow of inner light.
Through trials faced and paths unknown,
A steadfast heart, seeds of hope sown.

With every step, a promise made,
In shadows deep, we will not fade.
Dedication shines like the sun,
Guiding us till the work is done.

Through storms that test the strongest will,
Our spirits rise; they never chill.
In every struggle, find the spark,
A beacon bright in the dark.

So let us cherish this warm embrace,
In dedication, we find our place.
With open hearts, we pave the way,
For brighter dawns in each new day.

Sowing Seeds of Passion

In fertile ground, we cast our dreams,
Nurtured by hope, watered by beams.
Each seed a story, waiting to grow,
In gardens lush, where feelings flow.

With every touch, the earth responds,
Awakening spirit, making bonds.
Passion blooms in the gentle rain,
A tapestry woven through joy and pain.

Through golden fields, our laughter rings,
In moments shared, the heartache stings.
With every harvest, joy we reap,
In passion's cradle, we find our keep.

So scatter seeds where love can thrive,
In the rich soil, our souls alive.
For life is rich where hearts are worn,
In every passion, a new day's born.

The Canvas of Commitment

On a canvas blank, we start anew,
With colors bright and visions true.
Each brushstroke whispers tales of heart,
In commitment's hue, we play our part.

With steady hands, we build our dreams,
Crafting moments, or so it seems.
In shadows deep, our hopes reside,
The canvas wide, a joyful ride.

Through trials faced, we find our way,
In every challenge, strength will stay.
With every layer, truth appears,
A work of art through joy and tears.

So let us paint with fervent care,
In commitment deep, we find our air.
For life's grand masterpiece unfolds,
In every heart, a story told.

The Rhythm of Rewarding Tasks

In the morning light we rise,
Unfolding dreams that sparkle bright.
With each step, the spirit flies,
As effort turns to pure delight.

The world awaits our focused drive,
With passion fueling every move.
In this rhythm, we truly thrive,
As we navigate and improve.

Moments woven, finely spun,
Each task a thread in life's grand scheme.
Through challenges, we learn to run,
And find the strength to chase our dream.

Celebrate the path we tread,
For every struggle bears a gift.
In each milestone, joy is spread,
And spirits soar, our hearts uplift.

Sowing Seeds of Satisfaction

Underneath the vast, blue sky,
We plant our hopes, with care and love.
As seasons change, our dreams will fly,
With patience, they will rise above.

Each seed sown bears potential bright,
With effort, nurturing hands provide.
In darkened soil, we find our light,
Roots intertwine; no need to hide.

From humble ground, we watch them grow,
Flourishing with every chance.
In winds of change, our spirits flow,
Embracing life's enchanting dance.

Harvest time brings forth the prize,
With joy and gratitude in tow.
For every challenge, let us rise,
And reap the seeds of what we sow.

The Glow of Fulfillment

In the quiet of the night,
A gentle warmth begins to bloom.
As dreams align with heart's delight,
The glow of joy dispels the gloom.

With every step, we find our place,
A tapestry of moments bright.
Fulfillment dances, leaves a trace,
In every heartbeat, pure and light.

The laughter shared, the tears we've shed,
Remind us of this cherished space.
With open hearts and minds, we tread,
On paths that weave a warm embrace.

As starlit skies adorn the night,
We carry dreams into the dawn.
In the glow, we find our flight,
With courage deep, we all move on.

Echoes of Inspiration

Whispers ride the winds of change,
In every heart, a spark ignites.
Ideas dance, both bold and strange,
Fueling paths of rich insights.

In every corner, voices call,
Encouragement to break the mold.
The echoes rise, inspiring all,
To share their dreams, to be both bold.

Though shadows loom and doubts may creep,
Together, we will find our way.
In unity, our spirits leap,
Transforming night into bright day.

Let passion's fire light the dark,
As dreams unfold, new stories begin.
With every step, we leave a mark,
In echoes of the joy within.

Milton Keynes UK
Ingram Content Group UK Ltd.
UKHW020703191024
449793UK00005B/35